The Border

Don Schaeffer

ISBN: 978-93-6354-071-2

First Edition: 2025
Rs. 200/-

Cyberwit.net
HIG 45 Kaushambi Kunj, Kalindipuram
Allahabad - 211011 (U.P.) India
http://www.cyberwit.net
Tel: +(91) 9415091004
E-mail: info@cyberwit.net

Printed at Repro India Limited.

Contents

The Border

Now I live
in a small place.
The spreading out,
and broad space,
even the impatient
restlessness are gone.
I have come
to a microscope.
Minutia is my
wilderness. And here
I find my adventures
in the quiet resting place
of adventure.
It is new and strange.
I come to the border
of the strange and as
I slip past now into
darkness find
moving living things.

A Discovery

I learned something
last night
when I was
all alone. No one
taught me
but I didn't
make the knowledge.
I figured out
how I could
love without owning.
It's just a formula,
a discovery in principle
that I can only remember
without a chance
to practice.

The Size of a Dream

I can come
very close to dreams
but never reach them.
The joy of the goal is just
too great for this world,
scaled for human tolerences.
I can state the goal,
aspire, see it wavering before me
but never touch it.
The journey ends
before I arrive.
The intensity of this world
is always less
than my unruley wishes.
Are wishes
beyond the reach of the world,
on the edge of a gasp?
Today I got to have
a frank talk with a dream.
I learned
how stubborn she is.

Sensory Analog

I open the door
to a mini wheat
and the inside is
music played on
boxes made
of grain.
Soft harmonies
from odd instruments
that make music
no ear is tuned to hear.
Bless the melody of
mini wheat. Bless the
silence it makes.

Swallowing the Future

The truth is
a line of phantasies
that turn to
rocks and flesh.
The pictures that
time releases are masks
that protect me from
what I am too weak
to know. I huddle
on my bed in a dream
of gentle realness.
And only surprise waits
with its preparation
cocked and ready. Are you
frightened? She asks me.
I am too early to be
frightened. I may dodge it
this time.

The Luck of the Draw

The earth or
nature or God
or whatever we
told stories about
somewhere in words
or frightened whispers
or laughter, are gentle
enough to make this
silent. We don't have to
hear the gurglings of
the evolving world.
The authors of the
world keep their true
names silent. We
don't have to
confront the real
earth until it fades.

A Ballet About Economics

Gisselle choses death
after a dance
or offers her life
to pay for the life of a lover
who did not earn it.

Gisselle did not take death
earnestly. Death was not
justly earned. It was cheapened
and stolen, carelessly taken
in bad bargain, life
given away, fainting
after a laugh.

Those people
didn't know
how to make deals
when value was high
so life was cheap.

Flotsam

I am a string.
I dangle. Somebody
dropped me off
and I lay here limp.
I never had a use,
not enough color.
And no one can tie me.

But they made me.
A factory willed it.
Cost them a penny.
They didn't smile.
They tossed me
where I lay.
And still obey.

Necessity Is the Mother of Invention

My lamp is fixed so I can't see things and.

Necessity is not the only mother of invention.

That's what microbes tell us. Plants don't move and they are perfectly fine. Why do microbes move? Many microbes don't move and are more than happy with that. They pass not moving to new generations. Moving requires a whole bunch of new stuff. It seems wasteful of energy if one is steeped in food.

The Battle With the Dreams

It was defendable
living in fictions.
And I could do it,
possibly earned it.
But even fiction
is unreliable
vanishing in a day.
I have
fantasies that don't care,
uncaring, unreliable
dreams, just when
I need them most.
Stubborn me.
I keep looking for
new dreams, two steps back.
I try to make the time.

Slight Tooth Ache

After I lost that one front tooth
my mouth said "well
we don't
need to keep this space blank
we need to make changes."
So the mechinary
of change turned on.

And the machinary of change
bends flesh.
And the bending of flesh
always hurts a little bit.

In time the workers of the body
will call a holiday

Time Travel

But this isnt
my real life is it?

It's too familiar. It's
rehearsed right,

play. The evening
slides quietly past.

Voices enter memory
before they harden.

It will be
real tomorrow

when the sun rises
and when the drizzle stops.

And the days
press together

into years, waving
banners.

Paradise

Cry cry I want you to
in sight of a hundred legs
yell it out, toward the end,
at the beginning of missing,
in defeat. Cry like a boy.
Let everybody hear you
as you sprawl
and your legs
spread.

Good News

The value of love stock
is rising as the temperature
gets colder. It now sells
for more than five dollars
a share. And there are
many more companies
who sell it by the heartbeat
or by the word. And the market
has modernized with automated
love booths in refrigerated
appetite builders
across the country.
Little portable squeezers
can be purchassed for pennies
and distribution is free.

Monica

To me
the new world
has female parts.
She has the anatomy
of secrets.
She frightens me
with her unexplored powers.
The new world
laughs
and calls my bluff.
She opens secrets
without revealing them.
She gives nothing away.
I steal what I can
but every revelation
hurts.

Time Travel

But this isnt
my real life is it?

It's too familiar. It's
rehearsed right,

play. The evening
slides quietly past.

Voices enter memory
before they harden.

It will be
real tomorrow

when the sun rises
and when the drizzle stops.

And the days
press together

into years, waving
banners.

Fearless Answers to a Question

The answers to
the biggest and simplest
questions are
already in our minds.
They start in our loins,
language we know
but are not allowed to speak.
Naughty images
that can't be turned to words.
I would make the words
at night, in the quiet,
not seen and not spoken:
codes to the dirt
where many riches hide.
We have the secrets
but are not allowed
to say them

85

As I slowly
break into crumbs and
feel the strange quivers
of disappearing. As
value slowly
drops to zero,
I slip into theory.
I make up lies,
lower my standards for truth
and bring to the world
open dreams.
This world makes it easy.
Most of the time
no one sees me.
I can be superman.

I can do madness.
I can recover from it
and even calm it.
Madness moves in me.
I don't need
always to be real.
It's a joy that I
live under the cover of death,
the endless freedom
even as my eyes still gleam.
Madness of a joyous kind is
as easy as music.

My Last Girlfriend

I keep reliving romance.
The dead mystery of it
never dies. It's a
hope generator. The machinery
never shuts off, nothing
can close that switch.
Memory is the
enemy of fact. It
makes tears, dying so
painfully in silence.

The Place of Value in a World of Fact

Some poetry
breathes fire
but cools before
it reaches inside.
Some poetry just
vanishes and makes me curse.
Words like these
are just spewed or leaked
then sit cold. Nothing
warms them. Some poetry
are ghosts before
they are born, sitting
cold in the box
that stores it.
Some poetry are
ghosts before they are born.
But they don't waste much.

A Pickle

I wanna
take my bongos
and go home.
I lost those bongos
a long time ago
and they vanished
even from humor
and the home too.
That leaves only
smiles and courage.
I don't like those.

Rehearsing

I have hidden under a mask of life
all my years, never met death in person.
I think at my first personal face-to-face meeting

I may be a player.

That doesn't mean I won't fear. I am afraid
of big and powerful things. This, nothing will
scare away. It is not capable of mercy.

When I See My Neighbors

When the poem slows me down
I breathe. I wait.
I see my neighbors

waiting for me to move.
But I can't. "Get out of the way"
they say. I try to roll over

in the rocks full of sand.
My way is small
I can't share it.

I don't know how to share it.
Trained to be alone, my selfishness
is habit. I mean nothing by it.

The Cost

At three-forty-five in the afternoon,
he showed up.
And there was something
outlandish about his uniform,
which I'm sure I
wasn't supposéd to note.

He was an
immediate burden to my eyes,
costly to see. He drew
something out of me
and didn't pay.

He toured the room
but it did not raise my hopes.
His presence pulled hope
out of me, attached by a
string to time.

He left after an hour
without speaking.
He only
glanced at me with smiles,
and said "good day,"
which made it worse.

Rehearsing

I have hidden under a mask of life
all my years, never met death in person.
I think at my first personal face-to-face meeting

I may be a player.

That doesn't mean I won't fear. I am afraid
of big and powerful things. This, nothing will
scare away. It is not capable of mercy.

www.ingramcontent.com/pod-product-compliance
Lightning Source LLC
LaVergne TN
LVHW090130160826
845673LV00016B/1288

* 9 7 8 9 3 6 3 5 4 0 7 1 2 *